# JOY

by Jane Belk Moncure
illustrated by Pat Karch

THE CHILD'S WORLD

ELGIN, ILLINOIS 60120

**Library of Congress Cataloging in Publication Data**

Moncure, Jane Belk.
  Joy.

  (What is it?)
  Summary: Describes the feeling we know as
joy and the things that make us joyful.
  1. Joy—Moral and ethical aspects—Juvenile
literature. [1. Joy. 2. Emotions] I. Karch,
Pat, ill. II. Title. III. Series.
BJ1481.M68 1982          179'.9          82-1131
ISBN 0-89565-224-2                       AACR2

# JOY

What is joy?

Joy is a happy feeling inside that
bubbles out in a smile when your
best friend comes to play.

Making the first snowman of the
year—that's joy!

And after you have been out in the
snow, joy is a cup of hot cocoa with a
marshmallow on top.

Joy is playing the drum in a
rhythm band.

And joy is Thanksgiving dinner
at Grandma's house.

When you go to a new school, where you don't think you'll have any friends, and then you see a boy you know, that's joy!

Joy is having a part in the Christmas program.

Joy is seeing the rainbow after
a storm—

and running barefoot on the beach
with the sand tickling your toes.

Joy is finding your kitten after she's
been lost for two days.

And joy is making a kite that flies
—and doesn't crash.

When you go to the zoo and walk a long way to see the giraffes and the zebras and the monkeys and the lions and *then,* you see a water fountain— that's joy!

Joy is when the kids are choosing
teams and your brother chooses
you to be on his side, even
though you're the smallest.

And joy is when you hold your baby
sister for the first time and she goes
to sleep in your arms.

When it's really hot and you've
worked hard to put up the tent,
joy is hearing Dad say, "Let's go
for a swim."

And joy is jumping into the lake!

When your mom and dad have been away on a long trip and they come home and hug you—that's joy!

Can you think of other joyful things?

## About the Author:

Jane Belk Moncure, author of many books and stories for young children, is a graduate of Virginia Commonwealth University and Columbia University. She has taught nursery, kindergarten and primary children in Europe and America. Mrs. Moncure has taught early childhood education while serving on the faculties of Virginia Commonwealth University and the University of Richmond. She was the first president of the Virginia Association for Early Childhood Education and has been recognized widely for her services to young children. She is married to Dr. James A. Moncure, Vice President of Elon College, and currently lives in Burlington, North Carolina.

## About the Artist:

Pat Karch has shared an art studio in Dayton, Ohio, with her husband for 35 years. She had a great deal of early exposure to art. She was one of six children, four of whom became commercial artists. She received her training at the Dayton Art Institute in Ohio and the Academy of Art in Chicago. Since that time, she has illustrated greeting cards, children's books, and catalogs. She is the mother of three children. She attributes her ability to pursue her career as an artist, while raising children, to her husband—''an understanding and helpful partner.''

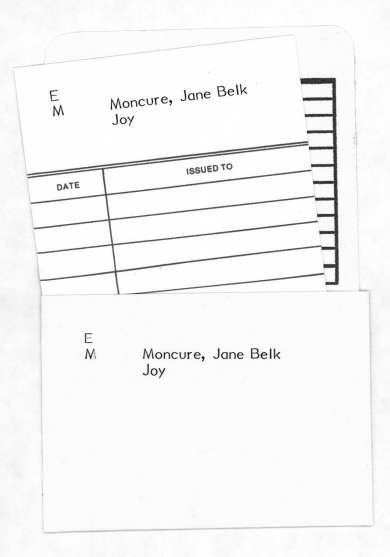

E
M       Moncure, Jane Belk
      Joy

| DATE | ISSUED TO |
|------|-----------|
|      |           |
|      |           |
|      |           |
|      |           |

E
M       Moncure, Jane Belk
      Joy